SPIRITUAL MIDWIVES

Hidden in the Earth
Called to Birth Out Purpose

Rosetta M. Parish

Staleon Group
Publications
ST. LOUIS • ORLANDO

Presented To:

_____

From:

_____

Date:

_____

SPIRITUAL MIDWIVES

Hidden in the Earth
Called to Birth Out Purpose

Rosetta M. Parish

Spiritual Midwives: Hidden in the Earth Called to Birth Out Purpose

Scriptures referenced: The Holy Bible, King James Version. New York: American Bible Society: 1999; Bartleby.com, 2000. All rights reserved. Used by permission.

Wikipedia contributors, "Midwife,"; "Caesarean Section,"; "Doula," Wikipedia, The Free Encyclopedia, en.wikipedia.org/w/index.php?title=Midwife&oldid=853000585; en.wikipedia.org/w/index.php?title=Caesarean_section&oldid=852672392; en.wikipedia.org/w/index.php?title=Doula&oldid=854123172 (All accessed August 11, 2018).

"Clarion Call," OED Online. Oxford English Dictionary. Accessed August 2018. http://en.oxforddictionaries.com/definition/clarion_call

Farrell, Heather. "Puah and Shiphrah," Women of the Scriptures, 12 August, 2009. Accessed August 11, 2018. http://www.womeninthescriptures.com/2009/08/puah-and-shiphrah.html

Higuera, Valencia and Healthline Editorial Team . "Premature Birth Complications: Short and Long-Term Health Effects.". Healthline, Healthline Media, 16 Dec. 2016. Accessed August 11, 2018. www.healthline.com/health/pregnancy/premature-baby-complications

Bohren, M. A., G. Hofmeyr, C. Sakala, R. K. Fukuzawa, and A. Cuthbert. "Continuous Support for Women during Childbirth." Cochrane. July 6, 2017. Accessed August 11, 2018. https://www.cochrane.org/CD003766/PREG_continuous-support-women-during-childbirth.

Mayo Clinic Staff. "Premature Births." Mayo Clinic. December 21, 2017. Accessed August 11, 2018. https://www.mayoclinic.org/diseases-conditions/premature-birth/symptoms-causes/syc-20376730

Child Development 12th Edition, Cram101 Textbook Reviews, Cochrane Database of Systematic Reviews 2003, Issue 3

Collier-Thomas, Bettye. Daughters of Thunder: Black Women Preachers and Their Sermons, 1850-1979. Jossey-Bass, 1998.

Front Cover Design by Ischa Gibson
Rear Cover Photography by Eddie Rhone, Jorhan Images
Rear Cover Design by Darrell Lobin

First Edition, 2018.
ISBN-13: 978-09-997880-3-5
ISBN-10: 0-9997880-3-5

Printed in the United States of America.

STALEON GROUP PUBLICATIONS
PO Box 592203
Orlando, FL 32859-2203
www.StaleonGroup.com

Staleon Group
Publications

Dedication

I dedicate this work to Elohim, the Creator. Thank you for giving me the gift of writing.

Contents

Foreward

Thanks to all those I encountered in life who took the time to share their struggles with me and allow the Holy Spirit to use me to put them into written words that will bless and encourage others.

Anything hidden has value and worth. The mere fact that time, space, and energy has caused a person, place, or thing to be moved from the viewing of the natural eye means, God has orchestrated it. God so beautifully takes his masterpieces, his treasures, and hides them in the earth and only He can reveal its location.

Prophetess Rosetta Parish has so wonderfully taken the student on a journey of discovery and how to locate a spiritual parent or midwife in the earth. The detail in which she unfolds each place in your life and the posture you should take to achieve all that God has is crucial to inhale. Many of the questions that plague the body of Christ about the role, the process, and the intimate godly bond between spiritual families are answered.

True Spiritual midwives are a rare commodity in the earth and find that their task is not greatly rewarded or honored at times. Often misunderstood and questioned it is a calling few can embrace.

Spiritual midwives find that they take on the role of labor and delivery and sometimes do not always have the joy of a continued role throughout the ministry of the spiritual son or daughter. Many times the birthing, the equipping, and training of spiritual sons and daughters are not discerned until the son or daughter are years into their personal ministries. However fulfillment comes for the Spiritual Midwife who captures in time what God preordained for purpose in each individual.

There is a longing in ones 'heart and soul to fill a void that only a spiritual parent can pour into. A pour that comes only thru like spiritual DNA. It is as the deep calling unto the deep with the wooing of the Holy Spirit as they administer and download destiny. As natural parents knows their offspring in a crowd, spiritual parents in like manner know those that are to be birthed from their loins.

"Again, the kingdom of heaven is like unto treasure hid in a field; the which when a man hath found, he hideth, and for joy thereof goeth and selleth all that he hath, and buyeth that field. Again, the kingdom of heaven is like unto a merchant man, seeking goodly pearls." (Matthew 13:44-45, KJV)

Spiritual parents are treasures hidden in the kingdom of God. It's takes a thirst and hunger for the original purpose of God to search them out. Many chose a lesser route. The longing to walk worthy of a call and make the election sure becomes insatiable without the midwife. When your son or daughter finally locates these treasures it is worth everything. Many have to choose between natural families, previous lifestyles, jobs, and etc. to sit at the feet of what God has interwoven. However it is worth giving up the entire field or ministry you once cherished.

Many stumble upon the spiritual relationship but find that it was divine eternal script that landed them in the path of a spiritual parent. Only this connection would unlock through the work of the Holy Spirit what God had preordained before time.

As you read this book ask the Holy Spirit to reveal to you true parents in Zion who will provoke the character of Christ, the zeal of the Lord, and fire of God from your life.

Me and my husband's ministry of being a Spiritual Midwives have been rewarding. We have birthed out over three hundred healthy sons and daughters over the past 20 years. Many of them are positioned in governmental and high ranking offices in the spiritual realm. *Producing and Promoting Healthy Leaders Through Mentorship, Fellowship, and Relationship"* (Dillon, 2011) has become our death process and our life process. It can never be replaced with money or buildings. However, the tabernacles that have erupted with power like Prophetess Rosetta Parish make being a hidden treasure found delightful.

Pastor Pamela K. Dillon

Agape Time Ministries-City of Refuge
Pastors John W & Pamela K. Dillon
Apostolic Founders & Gatekeepers

Introduction

As I began to put pen to paper and write this book. I began to compare a natural birth and a spiritual birth. I started to reflect on all of the people who took time to pour into my life. So, this book is dedicated to every mentor, pastor and friend that thought me worthy to invest your time in me.

I believe that midwives and mentors are missing in the Body of Christ. I had been in church all of my life, but I didn't have a relationship with God, meaning I wasn't intimate (closely acquainted) with Him until 2006. After starting a new job, I had an encounter with another employee who only worked part-time, about two days a week. After a brief conversation, she invited me to her annual Stir Up the Gift Conference, which later became the Stir Up the Gift Summit. My life has never been the same since that encounter. I am happy and honored to say that she became my mentor, along with her husband. I'm speaking of Pastor's John and Pamela Dillon. They are the people who taught me how to pray, stirred up my gifts, and launched me into my destiny.

"Who has heard such a thing? Who has seen such things? Can a land be born in one day? Can a nation be brought forth all at once? As soon as Zion travailed, she also brought forth her sons." (Isaiah 66:8, KJV)

At the end of the scripture, it states, "as soon as Zion travailed she brought forth her sons." Zion, meaning the church or body of Christ seeing that we meaning you and I are the church if we will cry out to God he would answer. I went to church for years not knowing my purpose or God's plan for my life. Until one day I was asked a question. Rosetta what is your assignment in the Earth?

As I began to seek the face of God to find out my purpose. I was introduced to my midwife John and Pamela Dillion who began to stir up the gifts in me that had laid dormant.

I would also like to say thank you to Bishop James A. Stewart, the person who saw the best in me even when I didn't. He walked with me until Christ was formed. He is an awesome teacher. I thank Elder Monica Bell for always making me stay accountable and always interceding for me. I thank Spiritual Midwife Apostle ILinda Jackson. I would like to thank Pastor Michael Johnson. Finally, I want to thank and acknowledge mentor and teacher Apostle Melissa Torre, a modern day spiritual midwife, skilled in the area of training and equipping individuals to carry their assignment full term by encouraging them and offering Godly wisdom.

Needless to say, I've had some awesome people covering and imparting into me and I am forever grateful.

So, to every Doula and every Midwife that labor to pour out purpose and push others towards their destiny, thank you.

Where are the Midwives

This generation of leaders need Spiritual Midwives to help mold, shape, and encourage them to walk in their destiny. They're yearning for guidance and instruction. We have all in the body of Christ. A *clarion call* has gone out.

CLARION CALL
Definition:
> **A strongly expressed demand or request for action.**
> **Clarion Call, Oxford English Dictionary**

People no longer want to just sit in church, not knowing their gifting or their purpose. They cannot afford to live any way they choose; continuing to believe everything is acceptable to God.

People want to see the Kingdom of God come to Earth and they want to walk with Kingdom Authority.

People need to know that their character, integrity and purpose matters.

Spiritual Midwives (male or female) have a great calling, to help us discover all of these things and birth out our purpose, but where are the midwives?

Spiritual Labor Pains

LABOR
Definition:
> **Toil, work**

PAIN
Definition:
> **Suffering**

I had been in church for years and not really knowing my purpose only knowing that there was more than I was giving to God and getting out of service.

The day I was asked what my assignment in the Earth was it sent me seeking to know my purpose.

I had spiritual labor pains for years, but when I began to seek God for clarity and direction I found myself being pushed towards my purpose.

To have a Spiritual Midwife that can see what you can't see about yourself is a blessing. Sometimes when you've been in labor for long periods of time you become too tired to push. Then the midwife must help you deliver. A Spiritual Midwife takes time to stir your gifts that have just laid dormant. So that you can reach your full potential in God when having spiritual labor pains, one can become frustrated, angry, and uncertain at times. The midwife encourages you reach your potential. I've discovered how we birth is extremely important. I have found that in this generation of leaders and ministers, we have forgotten those that pushed us into our purpose. I'm thankful for every person who has pushed, rebuked and love me into my purpose, so let's appreciate those midwives who labored with us to make Jesus known and not ourselves known.

The Spiritual Midwife

MID-WIFE
Definition:

> **A person (typically a woman) trying to assist women in childbirth. The Midwife is a trained help professional. Who helps healthy women during labor delivery, and after the birth of their babies. They specialize in pregnancy, childbirth, and postpartum.**
>
> **Midwife, Wikipedia.org**

Hidden in the earth, called to birth out purpose.

A Spiritual Midwife could be a mentor, life coach, Pastor, or even a friend.

The Spiritual Midwife generally sees the person's potential and are on an assignment to push it out of them. They have been assigned by God to stir up the person's gifts and launch them into their destiny.

A Spiritual Midwife gives strength to the person pregnant with purpose and vision by praying, encouraging and prompting them when to push.

They help with overdue Visions. Sometimes you can carry an assignment so long until your creativity and purpose has birth more and the carrier doesn't have what it takes to birth it out the Midwife steps in to assist by forcing (forceps) it to be birthed by urgent prayer, correction, love, and reassurance, however the Holy Spirit has instructed them.

The Spiritual Midwife must be an intercessor to stand in the gap for the person pregnant to make sure that the vision is not lost through miscarriage or aborted by lack of understanding of who they are.

The Spiritual Midwife has already been through the struggle of coming to know who they are. Their skilled in areas where the mentee / pregnant person is unsure. Their skilled in prayer, spiritual warfare, pulling down strongholds and deliverance.

Please Help Me Push

POEM

I keep feeling as if I'm in labor.

But every time I mention my pain I'm ignored

Yet the pain gets stronger and stronger

Begging to be attended to.

Will someone please assist me,

Please help me push?

I'm way past my due date.

I should have given birth to the purpose

The gifting I'm carrying,

To help someone else operate in what's inside of them.

My destiny is dying due to lack of healthy oxygen.

The Word of God states that I should Stir Up the Gift

Stir up,

Rekindle.

My fire has been dying

Due to lack of support;

Lack of understanding;

Rejection;

Self-doubt;

Shame of past mistakes.

But I have purpose growing

Lord, please send someone to help me push.

Where are the spiritual midwives?

Are they hidden in the Earth

Only to be revealed for such a time as this?

Purpose is Calling

Have you wondered why you're aggravated and agitated spiritually? Could it be that you are longing for more of the things of God, a deeper relationship with Him, and a need to know your purpose? Have you been praying for someone to help guide you? Does your heart have a longing that says, "God, I know that there is more to you than this!"

We are stuck attending service every week, going to program after program at Church, but no one's lives are being changed, no one is being delivered, because no one stopped to minister in the marketplace. This void must be filled with fresh oil, fresh Revelation, and a person to give instructions and directions.

Lord, please send me a midwife to help push out my purpose in the Earth birth. I have territory to take, lives to change, captives that are waiting to be freed. I hear my purpose assignment calling.

Are You the Next Spiritual Midwife

We know of some great women and men who have left their footprint in the earth, such as Katherine Kulhman, William Seymour, Maria Woodworth-Etter, Charles Parhan, Aimee Semple McPherson, and Mary Magdelena Tate, founder of the Church of the Living God, Pillar Ground and Truth, Inc. Where are the next midwives for this season? Will the Midwives please rise up, wake up, stand up and help others get up. To answer the call of purpose, destiny and ministry in their lives. The Body of Christ has need of you. Where are you? The lost, the broken hearted, the hurting, the rejected. They are waiting on you. They are waiting and waiting. Midwives arise and take your places. Where will you leave your footprint?

Two Midwives of the Bible

The Midwife who obeyed God, Puah and Shipra -Hebrew midwives:

But the midwives feared God, and did not ask the king of Egypt commanded them but save the men children alive. (Exodus 1:17, KJV)

The Hebrew word "obhnayim"(birth stool) is also used in Jeremiah 18:3, but here it is translated potter's wheel.

In this aspect the birthday store as regulates to potter's wheel I keep thinking of Jeremiah 18:3, when the Midwife is assisting a person instructing them to push, breathe Etc... It's as if they're on the "potter's wheel" being molded, shape, squeeze, Etc... All for the Masters use. (To Advance the kingdom.)

Puah and Shiphrah

Because they fear God more than man, God dealt well with the midwives and blessed them with houses. He prospered them.
Puah means Splendid in the Hebrew and Shiphrah means brightness.

Their lives were Splendid in full of brightness because they fear God more than men

The Hebrew term for birthstool in Exodus 116 AB 9 a.m. means literally two stones refers to primitive form of birth stool.

Source: http://www.womeninthescriptures.com/2009/08/puah-and-shiphrah.html

Caesarean Section

CAESAREAN SECTION
Definition:

> **A cesarean section (often c section) also other spelling is a surgical procedure in which one or more incision are made through a mother of abdomen and uterus to deliver one or more babies. A cesarean section is often performed when a vaginal delivery would endanger the mother or the baby's life or health risk. Some are performed upon risk request without a medical reason to do so.**
>
> **Cesarean Section, Wikipedia.org**

SPIRITUAL C-SECTION

Sometimes when a mentor, pastor, leader sees the potential in the person that they are called to mentor. They may be forced to make them deliver by spiritual caesarean meaning that they have to cause the gifting to come forth by spiritual surgery. They cut them spiritually by pressing them into prayer, fasting, cutting away everything that hinders them be it lust, unworthiness, doubt, lying down, self-doubt, rejection. They spiritually open up the core of the mentee by constantly speaking life and healing. They are able to point the mentee to their calling, even if the mentee can't see or believe it. While they are yet cut open, the wound in the light begins to heal them with love, confidence, joy, peace they begin to believe what was spoken to their Spirit when they were pregnant and uncomfortable with purpose. I myself have had mentors who understood who I was and what was on the inside of me even when I couldn't see it but yet they just kept pouring into me even when I tried to reject the instructions. I was spiritually cut open to give birth so I could live, love and lead. Please allow God to use and send people to do spiritual surgery on you. To truly be authentic a cesarean section might be necessary for purpose to be birthed.

Stillbirth

STILLBIRTH
Definition:
Stillbirth is the birth of a baby who is born without any signs of life at or after 24 weeks of pregnancy.

Why stillbirth happens? People think that many stillbirths happen because of a development or genetic problem that means the baby could not survive.

SPIRITUAL STILLBIRTH

Imagine carrying your gift, Talent, purpose but it comes forth with no sign of Life, all because you allow the umbilical cord of self-doubt to squeeze the life out of you. Yet you carry the vision full term but never thought to have regular checkups so you've looked healthy while pregnant but had no signs of life to bring forth the healthy baby.

The organs are of no use the heart, lungs, the eyes, Etc... The mind and heart, the seat of your emotions, has been deemed motionless Because we carried empty purpose, promises, goals, expectations and check out of life because you've been busy but non-active. You stopped showing signs of life from the spirit man. All because the gift you carry became lifeless the gift that was given by God that was to help others develop but it's arrived (D.O.A) dead on arrival because of Disobedience to God's voice, stubbornness and anger. Life of the purpose has no breath because lack of oxygen destroyed the purpose. That should have been used to bless others.

Birthing a Midwife

MIDWIFE TO MIDWIFE

Spiritual midwives called to birth out purpose. I thought about how a Spiritual Midwife could be birthing out a midwife. Doesn't matter if their male or female. It's just like God to connect people with like anointing and callings (not always) but sometimes it happens. I was told once by Pastor (Lizzie Stalling) you have to stop crying now because you're a spiritual mom now.

The Call for the Skilled (Male-Midwife)

In today's society we need more male-midwifes to help shape and mold the young men on how to serve God with no motive except to please God. They must learn in spite of their gifts their character must out shine their talent.

I happen to have come in contact with some awesome male midwifes who have shaped the lives of both male and females.
Bishop James A. Stewart, Pastor Michael E. Johnson, Apostle Eddie Stallings, Bishop Alton Davis Jr., Pastor B.A. Sanders and Pastor John Dillion, just to name a few.

To speak into the lives of others and leave a lasting impact that will cause others to change the direction, find the path they choose is a blessing. These men have caused many lives to be changed mainly because they listened, prayed and pushed others toward their purpose. The importance of a spiritual father in a person's life speak volumes. So, I say keep mentoring, pushing, stirring up gifts, correcting and loving.

Where are the male-midwives of today?

Premature Birth

PREMATURE BIRTH
Definition:

> Premature birth occurs if birth takes place more than three weeks before the baby is due. Premature delivery can result short or long-term health effects, including breathing problems, heart or brain problems, or long-term complications, such as cerebral palsy, hearing or vision problems, or behavioral problems.
>
> **Premature Birth Complications: Short and Long-Term Health Effects, Healthline.org**

Here is a list of problems caused by premature birth: Kidney problems, difficulty filtering waste from the blood, producing urine, eliminating waste without extracting excess fluid, and infections. The immune system is weak. Just as there are complications in premature delivery in the natural, so it is with the spirit.

When an individual is birth prematurely generally they are out of the timing of God. They haven't taken time to be developed or they feel as if they have arrived to a level where they can no longer hear wise counsel. They have become drunk off of the applause of people. Just as the vital organs must be grown in a premature infant, so must character, integrity, and patience be developed. If not their development becomes tainted with toxic waste and unhealthy immune system develops due to disobedience, rebellion, lack of prayer, etc. They can no longer hear clearly because of waste from the system; they have been drawn away by their own lust. They are underdeveloped and handicapped by their unwillingness to be trained and developed. These are just a few complications of premature birth, birthed premature by those who lead just to fill a need.

There are times when people are birthed prematurely because there is a need/ position to be filled in the church. There are also times when a person is released to fulfill a work because of their qualifications. They seem to be trustworthy or because they can quote scripture and they are made a leader, but does this qualify them to lead? They have character issues that may be overlooked just to fill the seats in the pulpit but yet they contaminate others with their way of thinking. As leaders we can't be in a hurry to fill positions with unequipped people. God will hold us accountable. We should never pour into people who refuse to change but we should pray for them. We don't want to have a group of underdeveloped people in Leadership positions. We train and equip people to be plant shakers and they are equipped with the word of God. Let them be true servants first and they will be awesome leaders. Pay attention to the motives of why people are around you. Is it to assist you or sabotage you? Mature people lead. Premature people just appear to be making moves. Know your circle. The elements that develop the premature birth extended into adult development growth. Don't release people into ministry prematurely.

Doula

DOULA
Definition:

> Doula comes from a Greek word that means woman who serves or handmade. A doula provides information, physical and emotional support and advocate for women and their Partners during and after the birth process. Unlike other practitioners such as hospice nurses and midwives do is do not give medical advice or have clinic duties.

Doula is a constant presence she is always at the mother's side. A doula will wipe your brow and place a cool towel on your forehead.

Also known as a birth companion and post-birth support, a doula is a non-medical person who assists a woman before, during, and or after childbirth, as well as her spouse and or family, by providing physical assistance and emotional support.

Source: "Continuous Support for Women during Childbirth." Cochrane, Cochrane.org, July 6, 2017.

SPIRITUAL DOULA

A Spiritual Doula prays for you, encourages you, to keep pushing and keep the goal in mind. DO YOU KNOW WHO YOUR DOULA IS?

They're not a midwife because they can't assist in the delivering of what the person carries which is the gift of anointing, but the Doula can encourage the pregnant person to relax, massage the purpose inside of them by praying with them and keeping them focused on what's already ahead of them because the spiritual weight of what they carry is greater than the struggle and disappointment of what they see or feel. They support the process of developing and waiting.

Doula in the spiritual analogy:

A spiritual doula as it relates to God will be one who encourages you to become all that God has created you to be. They encourage you to stay the course and assure you that you will be victorious. They pray for you and assist with the task of building you up. Absent of spiritual surgery. A doula will wipe your brow and remind you to breathe.

STATISTICS

In the US, 1 and 10 babies is born prematurely each year. That's nearly 400,000 babies born to early.

Preterm birth rates are different from different racial and ethnic groups.

Preterm Birth Rates	Racial, Ethnic Group
13.3 %	African Americans
10.4 %	Native Americans
9.1%	Hispanics
9.0%	Caucasians
8.5%	Asians

What is preterm birth?

The goal of a healthy pregnancy is to deliver a baby at 40 weeks of pregnancy preterm birth is the delivery of a baby between 20 and 37 weeks.

Source: https://www.mayoclinic.org/diseases-conditions/premature-birth/symptoms-causes/syc-20376730

Breech Birth

BREECH BIRTH
Definition:

> **A breech birth is the birth of a baby from a breech presentation, in which the baby exits the pelvis with the buttocks or feet first as opposed to the normal head first presentation. And breech presentation, fetal heart sounds are heard just above the umbilicus.**
>
> **Child Development, Cram101 Textbook Reviews**

SPIRITUAL BREECH BIRTH

Spiritual Breech birth is when a mentee is developed, but in the wrong position. An under-developed a prayer life, a lack of fasting, and forgetting to study the Word of God leads to a Spiritual Breech birth. They have wobbly, spiritual legs, under developed lungs, and they are caught between the birth canal too long, causing lack of oxygen. They are spiritually stuck between obedience and purpose.

In order for the birth to happen, adjustments must be made. The midwife may use birthing tools to assist her or him in the delivery. Tools, such as fasting, praying, and studying the Word with the mentee are used to correct their birthing position. Midwives instruct their mentee to develop patience and steadfastness. They encourage them not to take off, full speed ahead, starting their ministry out of the order of God. Rather, the mentee should learn step by step from the Holy Spirit and take the time required to become spiritually developed and delivered in the correct position.

Are You Shaping the Next Midwive or Daughter Of Thunder?

Could you be birthing a woman like Amanda Berry Smith? She preached sanctification and Grace. She stood against church prejudice and kept proclaiming the word. Julia AJ Foote, born 1823 was a great preacher and a great example to women.

Rosa A. Horn, born December 2, 1880. In 1926 Rosa moved to Brooklyn, New York. Within that same year she formed the Pentecostal Faith Church. Maria Woodworthetter ordained her Pentecostal church. By 1934 the Pentecostal Faith Church was established in multiple cities.

Source: "Daughters of Thunder: Black Women Preachers and Their Sermons, 1850-1979" by Dr. Bettye Collier-Thomas.

These women were pushed, pressed and stirred up to walk in their call and purpose they had examples midwives and doula's we don't know their names because they were hidden in the earth.

MIDWIVES AND DOULA'S RISE UP.

The Midwife Who Assisted?

POEM

I'm praying for someone to guide me to my destiny.

Someone full of wisdom and knowledge.

Someone who can know my past and still push me into my future a midwife who understands that God has a great plan for my life.

I've cried and prayed for her or him to find me so they can assist me with this delivery actually the due date has already passed.

I become frustrated and aggravated with what's on the inside of me.

It has attempted to break forth but I have found I can't deliver alone.

I need someone who has already carried to full-term and can understand me.

Lord please send her or him to tell me when this comes full circle.

I will know that the ministry you've assigned me to was worth the wait.

Lots of prayer, fasting, studying and serving others has prepared me and the midwives just arrived to instruct me to push it out be it through correction, love, or on-the-job training.

The time has arrived for me to push it out.
It will be healthy because the midwife was healthy, healed and whole.
They carry full term and endured.
Their qualified to assist in the birthing process thank you God for the midwife.

That helps birth out purpose.

Perfectly Flawed

Filled with purpose but misunderstood having visions but brushed aside because surely God can't be speaking to you? The mistakes you've made and you're saying you're pregnant with witty inventions, big ideas? You better go pray again, my friend, you heard wrong. The strong is who God called not the person who always seems to fall, yet you keep hearing God calling you to stand up and proclaim his word. Lead others to him walk in Kingdom principles that's why the pain because you're the perfect witness, Mentor, life coach, why you ask because you're flawed.

"I came not to call the righteous, but sinners to repentance." (Luke 5:32, KJV)

Honoring Your Midwives

This chapter is very important to me. I'm a firm believer that you should honor the people who helped shape your life; the people that saw your gifts and potential before you did; and the people God assigned to your life to help you become who He created you to be. The mentor, Pastor, teacher that sees the good, bad and the ugly, yet they labor with us anyway. So here are the people who labored with me, some for years, some for months.

Bishop James A. Stewart, my father in the Gospel. No one else could have labored with me as much or as long as he and his wife, Emerine Stewart, did. They were there through my battle with depression and issues with my son. They always had an encouraging word and rebuke, if necessary. Bishop Stewart could always see where God wanted to take me and use me for the Kingdom, even when I couldn't always see where God wanted to take me. Others dismissed me he kept pouring into me the word of God and challenging me to be my best.

Then there is Elder Monica Bell, the person Bishop James Stewart assigned to mentor me. I know there were times she wanted to quit, yet she kept praying and pushing, correcting and encouraging me to pray, study and don't stop fighting.

A Prayer

Father,

I thank you for connecting me to the person or persons that you have called to mentor and stir up the gifts that you have placed inside of me. To help grow your kingdom, for such a time as this may I always remain faithful, available, teachable & reachable. I pray that I will leave a foot print in the earth that will cause positive change.

Amen.

About the Author

Rosetta M. Parish is a native of Michigan City, Indiana and currently resides in Saint Louis, Missouri. She is the mother of one son, Daniel L. Simmons. Rosetta attends the Saint Louis New Testament Church, under the leadership of Apostle Melissa Torres. Rosetta is the Overseer of the Wailing Women of Zion Prayer Fellowship and the Wings of Worship Banner/ Flag Ministries.

Rosetta Parish is the author of two other books, *Finding Water in the Desert* and *Who Am I Really?* Rosetta 's prayer is to impact the kingdom of God by leading others to have an intimate relationship with Him in prayer, praise and worship.